Lothar-Rüdiger Lütge

Proof of the Existence of God: Why a Conscious Creator Is the Only Explanation.

FSC
www.fsc.org
MIX
Papier aus verantwortungsvollen Quellen
Paper from responsible sources
FSC® C105338

Publisher:
BoD · Books on Demand GmbH,
In de Tarpen 42, 22848 Norderstedt
Printed by:
Libri Plureos GmbH, Friedensallee 273,
22763 Hamburg

ISBN: 978-3-7597-9685-1

Contents

Introduction

For centuries, the question of God's existence has stood as one of the most fundamental and, at the same time, most controversial inquiries in human history. Philosophers, theologians, and thinkers from diverse cultures have attempted to answer it, yet to this day, the widely accepted view remains that a definitive proof of God's existence is unattainable. The general consensus is this: no proof of God exists that is rationally compelling and universally accepted, nor is such proof likely to ever be found.

Modern and postmodern perspectives have firmly anchored this assumption. They propose that if God exists, He exists beyond the reach of human understanding, and any conviction regarding His existence ultimately rests on personal faith and subjective experience. From this viewpoint, a rational, clearly reasoned proof of God appears simply impossible. It is assumed that humanity, ensnared within the limits of its own perceptions and understanding, has no genuine opportunity to address the question of God in a logical, comprehensible manner.

But what if we were to question this assumption? What if it were possible to prove the existence of God in a way that is logically consistent, compelling, and understandable? In fact, there exists an argument that can accomplish precisely this – an argument grounded in the essential realities of life and consciousness, one that demonstrates that the existence of God is not only possible but necessary. By examining the foundations of our being – the phenomenon of life and the experience of consciousness – we can arrive at an insight that logically affirms the existence of a personal Creator.

In our argument, we rely on three central assumptions that anyone can grasp through personal experience and observable reality: the existence of life, the reality of consciousness, and the foundational principle that "from nothing, nothing comes." These are not merely abstract ideas; they refer to the most profound and directly experienced phenomena of our being. We all encounter life and consciousness as undeniable facts—not as illusions or mental projections—and we know from experience that everything that exists originates from something else. Nothing can come from absolute nothingness.

These three assumptions form the foundation of our inquiry, leading us to a compelling conclusion: there must be a conscious, living source beyond the material world that has brought life and consciousness into existence. As we will demonstrate, this source can only be a personal God—a being endowed with life and consciousness, who has willed everything that exists into being.

Through a clear and reasoned approach, we will examine these assumptions step by step to reveal their logical implications. It will become evident that life and consciousness cannot be reduced to mere material processes and that their existence inevitably points to a transcendent source. By tracing the path of our own existence back to its origin, we arrive at a proof of God's existence—a proof grounded in the fundamental principles of logic and experience.

Chapter 1

The Reality of Life and Consciousness

Life and consciousness are the most fundamental phenomena of our existence. Everything we perceive, understand, experience, or think takes place within a state of conscious being. Life is the foundation that makes our existence possible, and consciousness is the medium through which we experience and reflect upon that existence. But what exactly do these two terms mean? Why are they so central to our understanding of reality and existence?

First, life describes the state in which an organism exists, grows, develops, and interacts with its surroundings. Life is not merely a function; it is a state of being that radically differs from inanimate matter. It is more than the sum of physical processes, more than a biological mechanism—life is an expression of activity, a "self-movement," a dynamic condition that acts and reacts through its own internal force.

Consciousness goes even further. It is the ability to perceive oneself and the world, to think, to feel, and to be aware of one's existence. Consciousness is the "I am" in its deepest sense—a state of awareness that makes us aware of our individuality and uniqueness. Consciousness is not only the perception of the external world but also the experience of one's own thoughts and feelings, the knowledge of one's own existence. This "I am" is not an abstract concept; it is an immediate, living experience that forms the center of each person's being.

Life and consciousness, then, are far more than mechanical or random processes. They are the cornerstones of our existence, leading us to question the origin of our being. They cannot be reduced to mere physical processes because they are what we experience directly, and they lie at the very core of who we are. Life and consciousness are not theories or hypotheses—they are real, experiential, and indispensable foundations for everything we think and know.

There are philosophical and spiritual perspectives that regard life and consciousness as illusions—mere appearances lacking true substance or reality. This view is particularly found in certain branches of Buddhism and in Advaita Vedanta within Hinduism, which regard the self and individual consciousness as delusions (Maya) and locate ultimate reality in a transcendent, impersonal absolute where all distinctions and individualities ultimately dissolve.

But how convincing is this perspective? If we consider life and consciousness as illusions, we encounter a fundamental paradox: the perception of illusion itself would require a form of consciousness. If life and consciousness were merely deceptions, then the awareness of this deception would also be illusory, making the idea inherently self-contradictory. The conscious experience of life and existence cannot be an illusion, for it forms the basis of all our perceptions and knowledge. Without consciousness, we would have no means to distinguish illusion from reality—consciousness is the very condition that enables us to contemplate reality and illusion at all.

Furthermore, life and consciousness are not abstract concepts but real, experiential states. They are not mere mental constructs; they form the foundation of our entire existence. Awareness of our own existence—our feeling, thinking, and experiencing—is not a distant idea but an immediate fact that we cannot deny without falling into contradiction. Anyone who wishes to deny that they are alive and conscious must do so from a state of consciousness—a paradox that reveals that life and consciousness cannot simply be dismissed as illusions.

Therefore, the reality of life and consciousness is not merely an assumption but an absolute certainty. They anchor us in reality and serve as the medium through which we experience ourselves and the world. Life and consciousness are not deceptions or constructs; they are the fundamental facts of our existence, which we must recognize as true and real in order to comprehend ourselves and the world at all.

The reality of life and consciousness becomes especially evident when we consider their transmission to the next generation. Life and consciousness are not merely phenomena that exist within individuals; they are qualities that can be passed on—and only through life itself. In biological reproduction, life is conveyed through a kind of "division" or "cellular transmission" to new life. What causes the next generation to appear alive and conscious is not the result of an external, artificial process but the direct transmission of the living and conscious essence itself.

If life or consciousness were merely an illusion, a deception of the mind, this process of transmission could not take place. An illusion cannot pass genuine substance to another being—it lacks any core that could be reproduced. Life and consciousness, therefore, cannot be mere appearances arising from a purely mechanical interplay of matter and energy. They must be real and authentic, for only in this way can they endure through the process of reproduction in the material world.

Attempts by science to artificially create life and consciousness have repeatedly highlighted this truth. Machines, no matter how complex or seemingly intelligent, do not live and are not conscious. They operate according to pre-set mechanisms and routines, but they lack self-awareness, an individual "I," an experience of being. Consciousness cannot be artificially generated; it must stem from a source that is already conscious.

Thus, life and consciousness always arise from a living, conscious predecessor. They do not spontaneously emerge from inanimate matter; rather, they must come from something that already possesses these qualities. This shows that life and consciousness cannot be mere properties of matter. Matter may provide the medium in which life expresses itself, but it is not the source of life and consciousness themselves. Life and consciousness require a living, conscious source to come into existence—a source that must itself be alive and conscious in order to impart these qualities into the stream of existence.

Chapter 2

The Impossibility of Artificial Life and Consciousness Creation

The advances in science and technology over recent decades have revolutionized our understanding of the material world. Through the study of biology, chemistry, and physics, we have unraveled the building blocks of life in increasingly finer detail. Molecular structures, genetic codes, and biochemical processes that make life possible are now well known in many of their mechanisms. Yet, despite all these achievements, science has been unable to overcome a fundamental barrier: the creation of life and consciousness from inanimate matter.

Since the dawn of modern biosciences, humanity has sought to penetrate the principles of life so deeply that it would be possible to create life artificially. Countless experiments have been conducted in biology and genetic engineering to create living organisms from non-living components. However, while we can assemble organic molecules, no experiment has succeeded in generating truly living, conscious life from inanimate matter.

One example is the experiments in synthetic biology. Scientists have managed to replicate individual biological components, even artificially modify genetic material and synthesize DNA. Yet, the results have always remained biochemical mechanisms—processes that can be controlled in a laboratory but do not produce independent life or consciousness. These synthetic approaches demonstrate impressive technical capabilities, but they lack self-awareness, an individual "I," and in no way are alive in the true sense of the word.

At the same time, immense efforts have been made in computer science and robotics to develop artificial consciousness. Today, there are highly advanced machines and programs capable of processing information at incredible speeds, making decisions, and even “moving” within their environment. So-called "Artificial Intelligence" can solve complex problems and even simulate human-like behaviors. Yet, however “intelligent” or powerful modern machines may be, they lack one fundamental quality: consciousness. They have no inner experience, no sense of being, no self-awareness. They do not "know" that they exist—they simply follow programmed instructions.

This boundary, which so far appears insurmountable, provides a crucial indication that life and consciousness cannot be reduced to purely material or mechanistic processes. Neither the organic building blocks of life nor machine algorithms possess the capacity to be independently alive or conscious. The question remains: Why is it impossible to create life and consciousness artificially, even though we understand the material foundation?

The repeated failure of science to create life and consciousness from inanimate matter suggests a fundamental truth: the origin of life and consciousness does not appear to reside in matter itself. Despite all the advances in biology, chemistry, and computer science—and the detailed understanding of many mechanisms and structures that sustain life—science has not been able to generate the "spark" of life and consciousness. Why is this?

The material world is a world of mechanisms, of cause and effect, of physical processes that follow clear rules and laws. A molecule reacts to another molecule according to fixed chemical principles, and a computer processes data through a sequence of logical operations. Yet the essence of life and consciousness eludes this principle. Life and consciousness possess a quality that goes beyond pure mechanics: they have an inner dynamism, a capacity for self-preservation, self-awareness, and independent experience.

When one tries to reduce life and consciousness to the laws of matter, one inevitably encounters a boundary. Machines, however advanced they may be, always act according to external instructions and programming—they have no "inner" world, no autonomy in their experience. Within matter itself, in its molecules and atoms, there is no trace of consciousness or the capacity for self-awareness. When we experience life and consciousness, we experience not only material processes but something that transcends these processes: the ability to perceive them and to experience them as "I."

This distinction suggests that the life and consciousness we experience are not the result of a mere accumulation of material components. Rather, life and consciousness require a source that is itself alive and conscious—a source that not only possesses these essential qualities but also has the capacity to transmit them.

The fact that life does not emerge from lifeless matter demonstrates that matter alone is incapable of bridging the gap to the living or the conscious. Everything points to the idea that life and consciousness originate beyond matter, in a realm that is itself alive and conscious. The repeated failure of science to generate the spark of consciousness serves as a silent yet powerful indication that life and consciousness must stem from a transcendent source—a source that is itself alive

and conscious and capable of bestowing upon us the gift of life and perception.
The fact that science has so far been unable to create life and consciousness from inanimate matter leads us to a logical conclusion: life and consciousness have a source that lies beyond the material world. There is something within our being that cannot be explained or generated by material processes alone. If even the most advanced technologies and scientific insights are unable to produce consciousness or life from mere matter, we are left with the only plausible assumption: that the origin of these qualities must be found in a sphere beyond the material world.

This source must be both alive and conscious, for only something that possesses these qualities itself can impart them. This principle is evident in nature, where living beings arise only from other living ancestors. Life perpetuates itself; it cannot spontaneously arise from nothing or from lifeless matter. The same is true of consciousness: the capacity for self-awareness, reflection, and experience can only come from a conscious source that inherently possesses these qualities.

The existence of such a transcendent source is not merely a hypothesis but the only logical explanation left when we consider the failure to artificially generate life and consciousness. This source must be more than an abstract principle or cosmic energy—it must be conscious, alive, and creative to bring life and consciousness into existence and pass them on. Such a being can only be understood as a personal, living God who has not only brought forth the life and consciousness we experience but has also purposefully shaped them.

The realization that we are not merely composed of material components but are embedded in a transcendent, living reality leads us directly to a proof of God. For if life and consciousness can only come from a conscious, living source, then our very existence—our life and our consciousness—points directly to the existence of God. We live and are aware of our being because we originate from a source that is alive and conscious, a source that has called us into existence as conscious individuals.

Chapter 3

The Principle of "Nothing Comes from Nothing"

One of the most fundamental principles, regarded as an indispensable foundation in both philosophy and natural science, is this: "Nothing comes from nothing." This principle states that nothing can arise from absolute nothingness. Everything that exists must have a cause, an origin from which it has emerged. Something cannot simply exist without preconditions, without reason, without cause. This law of causality forms the basis of our entire understanding of reality and existence.

When we observe the world around us, we see a universe full of complex structures, full of order, full of life and consciousness. The existence of these things demands an explanation. Neither the matter itself, with its observable structures and properties, nor immaterial qualities like life and consciousness can have simply "come from nothing." The universe—with all its visible and invisible components—is no accident and no mere illusion. It is real and tangible, and its existence compels us to seek its cause.

If we take the principle "Nothing comes from nothing" seriously, we cannot assume that the universe and everything within it arose from absolute nothingness. Something must have set the first impulse, the initial spark, to bring the existence of space, time, matter, and life into motion. A creation, whether material or immaterial, requires a creative source—a source that has willfully and consciously brought being out of non-being.

This creative source cannot be part of the material world itself, as it would then be subject to the same laws and limitations it created. Instead, it must exist beyond the boundaries of space and time, beyond the material level, and yet possess the power and consciousness to bring the entire existence into being. It follows that the universe and everything within it require a transcendent, conscious source—a source capable of overcoming nothingness and calling something into existence.

To explain the existence of the universe and all things within it, it is not enough to speak merely of a "cause"—the source must also possess specific qualities to bring forth the life and consciousness we experience. A mechanical, unconscious process might create physical structures, but it could not bring about the fundamental qualities of life and consciousness. The source of creation must be conscious and alive, for only in this way can it impart these qualities.

If we imagine this source as a principle without consciousness or life—a principle that is purely mechanical or impersonal—such a source might set a material foundation, like a physical impulse. Yet, it could not bring forth the living, conscious experience that we find within ourselves. Life and consciousness are qualities that go beyond the mere arrangement of matter and cannot simply arise from impersonal processes. They embody a quality of "being" and self-awareness that presupposes a conscious, living entity.

Only a living and conscious being can possess the creative power to bring not only matter but also consciousness and life itself into existence. The source of all being must therefore have consciousness and life itself in order to infuse these qualities into creation. Without this living and conscious source, life and consciousness would remain inexplicable—they could not find their beginning within the chain of causes and effects, as they transcend mere matter and must be rooted in something that inherently embodies them.

The principle "Nothing comes from nothing" leads us to conclude that the source of the universe must be more than an abstract "First Principle." It must have the creative power and intent to bring life and consciousness into existence. It must be alive and conscious, for only a living and conscious being can bring forth the qualities of life and self-awareness that we experience. This source is not an impersonal principle or a random impulse but a being with the conscious power to call the entire creation into existence.

When we examine the nature of this creative source, logic inevitably leads us to the conclusion that this source is transcendent—existing beyond the material world and its limitations. The transcendence of this source means that it exists outside space and time and is not subject to the natural laws that govern our universe. Yet, this source is not merely a distant, abstract origin; it is active, creative, and has willfully overcome the state of "nothingness" to bring the universe into being.

The fact that something exists rather than "nothing" reveals that transcendence is not merely passive. The source actively chose to overcome nothingness and bring forth creation. This is more than mere emergence or a random event—it is a conscious act of will and power. The transcendence that overcomes nothingness is a creative force capable of choosing and shaping existence. Such a being is not only transcendent but also intentional and personal.

This creative origin, which overcomes nothingness and brings forth the universe with all its laws, life, and consciousness, can only be understood as a personal God. Only a personal, conscious God could possess the power and awareness to call something into being from nothing. This creation was no accident; it was a deliberate choice to prefer being over non-being.

In overcoming nothingness through creation, God not only brought matter into existence but also laid the foundation for life and consciousness—qualities that reflect His own conscious and living nature. This origin is not impersonal but filled with intention and meaning, and through creation, God has imparted His own transcendence into the world.

The triumph of a transcendent, conscious God over nothingness shows us that our existence has an origin and a purpose. We do not live in a random universe without meaning or purpose; we are part of a creation that originates from a conscious, living source. This insight not only provides an explanation for our life and consciousness but also offers a grounding for our being: we are here for a reason and by a conscious decision, anchoring our existence in a transcendent reality that connects us all.

Chapter 4

The Proof of God and Its Implications

The considerations we have explored so far lead us to a compelling conclusion: the existence of a personal God is the only logically consistent explanation for our being, our consciousness, and life itself. Step by step, we have examined the prerequisites necessary to understand the phenomenon of existence, and this analysis has inevitably led us to the realization of a conscious and living Creator.

Our argument rests on a logical chain of basic assumptions and conclusions:

1. The Reality of Life and Consciousness – We have established that life and consciousness are not illusions. They are real phenomena that not only connect us to the material world but also serve as the starting point for all our experience and understanding. Life and consciousness are foundational facts of our existence and cannot be explained merely as byproducts of material processes.

2. The Impossibility of Artificially Creating Life and Consciousness – Despite decades of scientific effort, it has not been possible to create life and consciousness from inanimate matter. This failure suggests that life and consciousness cannot arise solely through mechanistic, material processes but require a living, conscious source.

3. The Principle of "Nothing Comes from Nothing" – The existence of "something" instead of "nothing" requires a cause that is not part of the material universe itself. This cause must possess the creative power to bring being out of non-being. The principle of "Nothing comes from nothing" points us toward a transcendent source capable of calling the universe and everything within it into existence.

4. The Necessity of a Conscious and Living Source – To bring life and consciousness into existence, this transcendent source must itself be alive and conscious. Only a conscious, personal power could infuse the qualities of life and consciousness into creation.

From this logical chain, it becomes clear that the existence of the universe, life, and consciousness can only be explained by the assumption of a personal God. Such a God is not merely an abstract principle or cosmic force but a living, conscious being who has intentionally brought being into existence. This God is the origin of all that is alive and conscious and thus forms the foundation of our own existence.

The logical chain that has led us to the assumption of a personal God allows only one consistent conclusion: the existence of a conscious and living Creator is the only coherent explanation for our being. All other assumptions—such as the idea that life and consciousness are mere products of material processes or that the universe emerged from absolute nothingness—lead us into contradictions and ambiguities that are incompatible with our own perception of reality.

Modern science has produced many theories to explain the origin of the universe and life, yet none of these theories can truly grasp the origin of life and consciousness. The attempt to reduce everything to mechanisms of matter inevitably reaches its limits, as life and consciousness are not mere properties of matter—they are fundamental qualities that must stem from a living, conscious source. Without a transcendent, conscious cause, the existence of life and consciousness remains mysterious and incomprehensible.

If we take the principle "Nothing comes from nothing" seriously and recognize the phenomenon of conscious self-awareness, which we all experience, as a genuine reality, we are left with the insight that there must be a Creator who possesses the power and consciousness to bring forth life and consciousness. This Creator is not only the origin of matter but also the origin of being and meaning. He has not only called the world into existence but also imbued it with an inner order and purpose, which is reflected in our capacity for self-awareness and conscious experience.

Only a personal God who acts intentionally and consciously can be the cause of our existence and the source of the qualities that define us as conscious individuals. The existence of a personal God is therefore not merely a matter of faith but the only logical conclusion derived from the fundamental phenomena of life and consciousness. Our existence is neither a coincidence nor a mechanistic byproduct of material processes; it is a conscious creation that points to a personal God. This God is the ground and purpose of our being—the source that has brought forth all life, all perception, and all consciousness.

The realization of a personal God who has called our being into existence challenges the foundation of the modern and postmodern worldview. For centuries, modern thinking has been based on the idea of an autonomous human being, self-sufficient and understanding life and existence without reference to a higher, transcendent reality. This worldview positions humanity as the absolute center—a being capable of finding all knowledge and answers through its own power and intellect. But if we follow the logic of existence, as we have developed in the preceding chapters, it becomes clear that this assumption is mistaken.

Humanity is not the absolute center but part of a creation brought into existence by a higher, living, and conscious being. Without acknowledging this Creator, the modern worldview remains incomplete and unsustainable. It lacks a foundation on which it could truly endure. An autonomous worldview without a transcendent source leads to a mindset that ultimately reduces life and consciousness to mechanistic processes and chance, resulting in an existential emptiness. In such a worldview, humanity appears as a random phenomenon in a cold universe—without higher significance, without a true foundation, and without deeper meaning.

The modern and postmodern worldview is thus built on shaky foundations. It lacks the real substance that only a living, conscious Creator can provide. The notion that humanity is self-sufficient, that it can exist independently of a transcendent order and source, leads to a mindset of isolation, nihilism, and ultimately disorientation. The person who sees themselves as an autonomous being loses the anchoring that provides stability and meaning. As modernity shows, this leads to an inner emptiness that is difficult to overcome.

A worldview that seeks to explain life and consciousness without a conscious, living source misunderstands the deepest nature of being human and denies recognition of its own roots. The assumption that we need neither a higher source nor a transcendent goal has led us to an era where direction and purpose often seem lost. Yet, the realization of a personal God as the source and foundation of our existence offers a path that transcends mere rational and mechanistic thinking—a path to a more fulfilling, deeper, and truer existence that is aware of its roots and its purpose.

Only through the insight into the reality of a conscious, transcendent source can the human worldview become complete and sustainable. Acknowledging a personal God leads us to a worldview that comprehends life, consciousness, and humanity in their full depth, granting them their rightful place in creation—as conscious, independent creations of a living God.

Chapter 5

The Consequences of a Transcendent Creator

The realization that our being is rooted in a conscious, transcendent Creator is not merely an intellectual conclusion—it has far-reaching ethical and existential implications. If we assume that our existence is no accident but the result of intentional creation, then our lives take on a new dimension: they hold not only substance but also a deeper meaning and a responsibility that goes beyond personal autonomy.

A transcendent Creator who has deliberately called life into existence did not create us arbitrarily or thoughtlessly, but with purpose and intention. This realization fundamentally changes our understanding of morality and responsibility. Ethics, then, is not merely an agreement that people make for social living; it is an expression of a higher order grounded in the will of the Creator. Moral principles and ethical norms, in this light, are not relative or negotiable but absolute and binding—they reflect the Creator's intention and law, which apply to all people.

Moreover, this insight endows our lives with meaning that is independent of external circumstances or subjective desires. We are not merely individuals existing for ourselves; we are conscious beings placed within a God-given order. The relationship to a transcendent Creator calls us to understand our existence not only as personal freedom but also as a responsibility. This responsibility encompasses both our actions toward others and our attitude toward life itself. Our lives are a gift that we are meant to care for and respect—not for selfish benefit, but as an expression of reverence for the Creator who has called us into existence.

The consequence of this realization is far-reaching: if we are part of a conscious creation, then our lives are inseparably connected to the intent of this Creator. This insight gives our existence a depth that goes beyond mere personal self-fulfillment. It calls us to live in harmony with the principles that align with the Creator's will and to see our lives as part of a greater order.

The realization that our being is rooted in a conscious, transcendent Creator challenges our current ways of living and thinking. In many respects, the modern world lives and thinks as though there were no divine origin or higher order. Humanity sees itself as autonomous, independent, and free, with no reference to a transcendent source. But this self-perception leads us into a state comparable to "mutiny"—a rebellion against the natural, divine order that fundamentally supports and guides our existence.

This mutiny manifests itself in many ways. The modern way of life is often marked by the notion that humans are the creators of their values and the meaning of their lives. The idea that ethical norms and principles of life are merely social constructs or individual choices denies the possibility of a universal, divine order. In place of binding values, we see flexible, subjective norms that adapt to personal preferences and momentary majority opinions. This leads to a state of moral arbitrariness, where the pursuit of individual benefit and comfort takes precedence over the principle of a universal, divinely grounded ethos.

This state of "mutiny" is essentially an expression of the refusal to recognize one's existence as part of a greater order. By distancing itself from the idea of a divine origin, humanity creates a way of life that, in practice, amounts to a denial of its own roots. Rejecting a divine origin leads to a self-concept in which humanity sees itself as self-sufficient, with no higher purpose or responsibility to fulfill. This departure from divine order is not without consequences: modern society suffers from a loss of direction, meaning, and inner stability—a deficit that often manifests as personal or societal crisis.

If we extend the metaphor of "mutiny," it also suggests that humanity has placed itself in a state of turmoil and inner unrest. Like sailors who have overthrown their captain and are adrift on an endless sea, modern humanity finds itself facing the emptiness and disorientation of an existence detached from its origin. Without acknowledging a divine order, there is no reliable direction, no compass that grants life a deeper meaning. Humanity becomes the supposed master of itself, yet without a true foundation for this freedom. People are free, but this freedom is, in reality, an unmoored state that leaves them uprooted and directionless.

The mutiny against divine origin and divine order may appear as freedom, but it leads us into an existential no-man's-land where the true nature and higher purpose of our existence are obscured. In this sense, the modern world represents not only a detachment from traditions or belief systems but also a profound, systematic denial of the truth underlying our being. The consequences are a loss of meaning, stability, and community—an inner emptiness that no external freedom or self-fulfillment can fill.

The realization of a transcendent Creator who has called us and the entire universe into existence is more than an intellectual conclusion—it is an invitation to view our lives and being in a new light. The modern world has taught us that we are independent and autonomous, self-sufficient beings, but this belief has led us into inner emptiness and disorientation. Returning to the truth of our divine origin offers us the chance to fill this emptiness and to see ourselves as part of a larger, meaningful whole.

Living in accordance with divine order is not a loss of freedom but a return to our true nature and purpose. By acknowledging the God-given order and accepting it as part of our own being, we experience a freedom that transcends mere choice or action. This freedom is rooted in an inner foundation, a clarity about who we are and why we exist. It gives our lives a direction and meaning that endure, regardless of external circumstances.

This return to divine order does not mean that we must follow a rigid set of rules; rather, it invites us to see our existence as part of a greater truth. The divine order is the expression of the will of a personal, living God who loves life and has brought His creation into being with purpose and love. It offers us an anchor that provides stability even in the storms of life, a foundation that fills our lives with a purpose and meaning that go far beyond the here and now.

We are invited to understand our lives as part of a creation rooted in a conscious decision by God. This realization not only provides us with stability but also inspires a perspective of reverence and gratitude. It calls us to act with mindfulness and responsibility, to care for our existence, and to live in harmony with divine order. By acknowledging our divine origin, we step out of isolation and disorientation and find ourselves within a relationship—with God, with others, and with all of creation.

This invitation to return is ultimately an invitation to personal reflection: What does it mean to live in a world brought into being by a conscious Creator? What responsibility does each of us bear in light of this truth? And how can we shape our lives in alignment with this divine order? The answers to these questions will differ for each person, yet they lead us all to a deeper insight into the meaning of our existence and the truth that, as conscious, beloved creations, we are part of a larger, God-given context.

Conclusion

A Path Out of Emptiness

The realization that our lives are grounded in a conscious, personal Creator offers a way out of the emptiness and disorientation that so many people feel today. This insight is not a restriction of our freedom; rather, it is a return to the truth of our existence—a truth that provides stability, meaning, and a profound grounding in being. The idea of a personal God who intended and loved us before we existed is a return to an order that is neither alien nor overpowering, but an order in which we, as living, conscious beings, can find ourselves and fulfill our potential.

In a world that often pushes us to view ourselves as autonomous and isolated individuals, the recognition of a divine origin brings us back to our innermost self. It offers an answer to questions about the meaning, purpose, and value of our lives. This return to divine order is not a loss of self-determination; rather, it is a way to discover and realize our freedom in its truest depth. By aligning ourselves with the larger context of the divine will, we gain a freedom founded on truth, leading us to a fuller, more fulfilling existence.

God did not create us as machines or robots, blindly following His commands. Instead, He endowed us with consciousness and free will, enabling us to make our own decisions: we can turn away from Him and follow our own path, or we can turn toward Him in friendship and love. This free will, this gift of consciousness, makes us autonomous beings capable of seeking and finding God of our own accord. It is likely that God desires precisely this voluntary turning toward Him—a turning rooted in love and in the recognition of the truth of our existence.

In this context, our free will takes on a special significance. Love and friendship are only genuine and profound when they are given freely. God "had" to endow us with consciousness and free will to make such a relationship of love and friendship between Himself and His creations possible. Perhaps He waits for us to use this freedom to return to

Him out of our own understanding. The Christian parable of the prodigal son illustrates this beautifully: God, as the father who waits eagerly and runs to embrace his returning son, is a powerful image of the relationship God seeks with us—not a forced return, but a voluntary, conscious decision to come back to our divine source.

This invitation to return is also an invitation to true freedom and the fulfillment of our deepest purpose. By turning to God in love and friendship, we enter into a relationship that takes us far beyond what we can achieve as mere individuals. It is a step back into a connection that not only strengthens our inner peace but fills our entire existence with meaning and purpose.

Appendix

The Logical Steps of the Proof of God's Existence, Presented in Summary:

Step 1: The Reality of Life and Consciousness

Core Statement: Life and consciousness are real phenomena, not illusions or mere products of matter.

Conclusion: Life and consciousness require a source that itself possesses these qualities.

Step 2: The Impossibility of Artificial Creation

Core Statement: Despite all scientific efforts, life and consciousness cannot be created from inanimate matter.

Conclusion: Life and consciousness are not reducible to mechanical processes and require a conscious source.

Step 3: The Principle "From Nothing Comes Nothing"

Core Statement: The existence of something (whether material or immaterial) requires a cause and cannot emerge from nothing.

Conclusion: The universe requires a creative source that called being into existence from non-being.

Step 4: The Necessity of a Conscious Source

Core Statement: Life and consciousness can only arise from something that is itself conscious and living.

Conclusion: The source of life and consciousness must be conscious and alive—a being with will and intention.

Step 5: The Existence of a Personal God

Core Statement: A conscious and personal God is the only logical explanation for the universe and our existence.

Conclusion: Our existence is founded in a conscious, living Creator who brought life and consciousness into being.

Other texts by the same author.

In English:

A Conscious Choice for Faith
The Deliberate Return to God as Salvation from Crisis

BoD Verlag, 2024
ISBN 978-3-7597-9494-9

The Veneration of the Blessed Virgin Mary
A guide to understanding the Mother of God for reformed Christians and people of other faiths.

BoD Verlag, 2023
ISBN: 9 783757 830595

In German:

Bewusstsein, Individuum, Gott
Ein offener Dialog

BoD Verlag, 2024
ISBN 9 783 769 303018

Entscheidung für den Glauben
Die willentliche Rückkehr zu Gott als Rettung aus der Krise.

BoD Verlag, 2024
ISBN 9 783759 785060

Die Architektur des Glaubens: Weltbilder und ihre Auswirkungen
Die Rolle des Theismus und des Christentums in einer fragmentierten Welt.

BoD Verlag, 2023
ISBN 9 783757 890032

Gott ist Person!
Warum es wichtig ist, Gott als ein ewiges, unveränderliches Individuum zu begreifen.

BoD Verlag, 2019
ISBN 9 783744 820004

All publications are available in paperback and e-book format.